# When Words Combine

Word Puzzles
by
Mark Van Horne

≈ Mattabesset ≈

mattabesset@gmail.com

ISBN: 978-0-9714221-3-1

Thanks to J, L and S

# Contents



Can you find the hidden puzzle?

# Introduction

I thought you might enjoy a book of puzzles about words made with other words—about words combined. Most of the combinations you'll be playing with here are familiar types: compound words like *dishwasher*, hyphenated words like *part-time* and two-word phrases like *movie star*.

But some of the combinations you'll encounter here were not created that way intentionally. These are unplanned, inadvertent combinations such as *massage* (mass+age) and *beam* (be+am). You'll get to have some fun with words like these in the Unintended Combo sections.

Each chapter has a different type of puzzle, though they are all variations on the same theme. Each chapter begins with a description and has an example to get you off to a good start.

You probably won't need paper and pencil to solve most of these puzzles. Of course, you can use them if you want.

I hope you find this collection entertaining and challenging. I welcome your comments; please feel free to contact me. Now, let the *divers+ions be+gin*.

Mark Van Horne
vanhorne.mark@gmail.com

# 1

# Make a Chain

Each puzzle in this chapter starts out as a list of five words. It's up to you to arrange and combine these words into a connected chain of four new words. To do this, take two words at a time and make a single new word. It can be a compound word, a hyphenated word or a two-word phrase. Arrange them so that the last part of one is also the first part of the next one in the chain.

Here is an example:

cake
cup
out
tea
walk

After combining and rearranging, here is the chain:

teacup cupcake cakewalk walkout

So, you see how it works? OK, go ahead and give it a try.

# Make a Chain 1

pie
pot
wise
other
crack

Answer on Page 128

otherwise wisecrack
crackpot pot pie ✓

# Make a Chain 2

pop
silk
corn
worm
soda

Answer on Page 129

sodapop
popcorn
silkworm
corn silk

sodapop popcorn cornsilk silkworm ✓

# Make a Chain 3

sugar
root
brown
cube
cellar

Answer on Page 130

brown sugar
sugar cube
cube root

brown sugar sugar cube
cube root root cellar

# Make a Chain 4

mine
ball
salt
hand
field

Answer on Page 131

saltmine

handball

mine field

field hand

saltmine minefield field hand
handball ✓

# Make a Chain 5

side
way
any
road

Uh-oh. One of the words in the list has gone missing. But it's around here somewhere.

Answer on Page 132

roadside wayside
anyway

# Make a Chain 6

their
bear
sow
four
owe

This doesn't look quite right. I dictated this list and my automatic spell check must've made some poor choices. Please correct the spelling and solve. Thank you.

Answer on Page 133

forebear
therefore

# Make a Chain 7

~~angle~~ ~~back~~ low
front ~~right~~ ~~cut~~
lie up ~~down~~ runner

Oops! Two chains are tangled together. Please sort them out.

~~low cut~~ lie low

Answer on Page 134

up front ~~back down~~
~~lie back~~ front runner
~~down right~~ ~~low down~~
runner up ~~upright~~
~~cut up~~ ~~right angle~~
~~cut back~~

X

cut back back down
down right right angle

lie low low front
front runner runner up

# Make a Chain 8

stop
turn
eat

Due to budget constraints, one word is used twice. Unfortunately, that particular word is missing.

Answer on Page 135

# Make a Chain 9

hold
par
hand
over
under

Ahh! Back to normal. Let's hope there will be no more nonsense in this chapter.

Answer on Page 136

under par
underhand
handover
over par
hand hold
hold over

# Word Chain Fill-ins

Each puzzle in this chapter is a word chain with two words missing: the second and the fourth. Your task is to figure out what these words are and restore the chain.

As a special feature, these two missing words link to each other to form a familiar word or two-word phrase. Also, the first few puzzles have a hint for the missing words.

Here is an example with the hint already provided:

egg ? hot ? chip

Hint: light confection

Answer: The light confection is *white chocolate*. Put *white* in the first space and *chocolate* in the second space to get this chain:

egg white white hot hot chocolate chocolate chip

Please remember that hyphenated words and two-word phrases are acceptable. Thank you for your kind attention; you may now proceed.

# Fill-in 1

dry ? cold ? puff

Hint on Page 120

Answer on Page 137

dry ice ice cold cold cream
cream puff

# Fill-in 2

red ? bed ? break

Hint on Page 121

Answer on Page 138

# Fill-in 3

touch ? under ? mate

Hint on Page 122

Answer on Page 139

touch down down under
underplay playmate ✓

# Fill-in 4

winter ? tea ? broken

Hint on Page 123

Answer on Page 140

# Fill-in 5

flower ? spread ? music

Hint on Page 124

Answer on Page 141

flower bed bedspread
spreadsheet sheet music

# Fill-in 6

fish ? hand ? pat

Hint on Page 125

Answer on Page 142

# Fill-in 7

saw ? eye ? paste

Answer on Page 143

# Fill-in 8

over ? desk ? hat

Answer on Page 144

# Fill-in 9

face ? board ? point

Answer on Page 145

# Fill-in 10

midnight ? • ? weight

Answer on Page 146

# Fill-in 11

wide ? ? code

Answer on Page 147

# Fill-in 12

side ? stall ? shoot

One of the given words is a synonym of the actual word and has the same number of letters.

Answer on Page 148

# Unintended Combo Fill-ins

These puzzles are similar to the previous ones in that the second and fourth words of a chain are missing and it's up to you to fill in those blanks and restore the chain.

The main difference here is that these chains are made of Unintended Combos, words made of smaller words not related to the larger word's meaning. For example, *garbage* is an unintended combo made from the two component words *garb* and *age*, neither of which has anything to do with the meaning of garbage. Well, unless you're complaining about the old clothes I wear around the house.

Another difference from the previous chapter is that the two missing words do not link to each other.

Here is an example of an Unintended Combo Fill-in:

sea (3) net (3) ring

Think of two component words of the indicated lengths. The first one makes a word when added to the end of *sea* and another word when placed at the beginning of *net*. The second component should make words when put at the end of *net* and the beginning of *ring*.

Answer: the two missing component words are *son* and *her*. The restored chain is

season   sonnet   nether   herring

All of the component words in this chapter have at least two letters. The first few puzzles show the number of letters in each component word but the ones after that have only question marks to indicate the missing words. And the puzzles after that have only a list of three words and you must arrange them into the correct order and supply the missing components.

Well, this is a lengthy explanation, isn't it? Let's end all this wordiness and get on to the, um, word stuff.

# Unintended Combo Fill-in 1

fun (4) bat (2) art

Answer on Page 149

# Unintended Combo Fill-in 2

see (3) me (3) hem

Answer on Page 150

# Unintended Combo Fill-in 3

ram ? her ? evil

Answer on Page 151

# Unintended Combo Fill-in 4

car ? ten ? ate

Answer on Page 152

# Unintended Combo Fill-in 5

oil
caps
doors

Answer on Page 153

# Unintended Combo Fill-in 6

me
do
rely

Answer on Page 154

# Odd Word Out

Each puzzle in this chapter consists of a list of four words. Three of the words have something in common: they can be combined with some other word to make a new word—a compound word, hyphenated word, or two-word phrase. (The next chapter uses Unintended Combos.) It's up to you to think of that other word and determine which one of the words in the list does not belong. The word that does not belong has the same number of letters as the companion word you must think up.

For example, given this list:

free
helping
self
some

the word that does not belong is *self* because the other words can be combined with *hand* to make *freehand, helping hand* and *handsome.*

And now, whether or not you think I am handsome, I invite you to help yourself freely to the puzzles in this chapter.

# Odd Word Out 1

dog
north
stop
tower

Answer on Page 155

# Odd Word Out 2

fuel
block
pipe
stem

Answer on Page 156

# Odd Word Out 3

bar
box
milk
power

Answer on Page 157

# Odd Word Out 4

ball
data
line
park

Answer on Page 158

# Odd Word Out 5

catch
land
mud
show

Answer on Page 159

# Odd Word Out 6

barrel
engine
party
strip

Answer on Page 160

# Odd Word Out 7

down
heart
house
muscle

Answer on Page 161

# Odd Word Out 8

bath
brain
jail
time

Answer on Page 162

# Odd Word Out 9

cow
hard
straw
trick

Answer on Page 163

# Odd Word Out 10

fly
sand
stone
weight

Answer on Page 164

# Odd Word Out 11

eye
key
prime
spare

Answer on Page 165

# Odd Word Out 12

hay
pitch
ranch
yellow

Answer on Page 166

# Odd Word Out 13

home
fashion
party
working

Answer on Page 167

# Odd Word Out 14

moth
gown
fire
wick

Answer on Page 168

# Odd Word Out 15

quarter
back
magic
sense

Answer on Page 169

# Odd Word Out 16

main
test
crash
lady

Answer on Page 170

# Odd Word Out 17

chain
fan
order
yard

Answer on Page 171

# Odd Word Out 18

meet
shark
sound
off

Answer on Page 172

# Unintended Combos
# Odd Word Out

As in the previous chapter, your task is to think of a word that can be combined with three of the four words in each puzzle. Also as before, the word that does not belong has the same number of letters as the answer word. The difference here is that all the combinations are of the unintended variety.

For example, given this list of component words:

band
dig
elf
oar

the companion word is *its*, making the new words *bandits*, *digits* and *itself*. The word that does not belong is *oar*.

All of the companion words in this chapter have at least two letters. Enjoy!

# Unintended Combos
# Odd Word Out 1

has
pan
sting
tapes

Answer on Page 173

# Unintended Combos
## Odd Word Out 2

less
or
so
us

Answer on Page 174

# Unintended Combos
# Odd Word Out 3

end
fit
nest
then

Answer on Page 175

# Unintended Combos
# Odd Word Out 4

bode
ping
set
to

Answer on Page 176

# Unintended Combos
# Odd Word Out 5

he
man
sling
tan

Answer on Page 177

# Unintended Combos
# Odd Word Out 6

corn
just
off
tin

Answer on Page 178

# Unintended Combos
# Odd Word Out 7

hum
war
post
stub

Answer on Page 179

# Unintended Combos
## Odd Word Out 8

fur
spar
cat
dies

Answer on Page 180

# Unintended Combos
# Odd Word Out 9

tally
ace
ton
swear

Answer on Page 181

# Unintended Combos
# Odd Word Out 10

mist
dam
thresh
outs

Answer on Page 182

# Unintended Combos
# Odd Word Out 11

the
sins
vest
force

Answer on Page 183

# Unintended Combos
## Odd Word Out 12

rear
itch
since
amen

Answer on Page 184

# Unintended Combos
# Odd Word Out 13

let
each
act
rove

Answer on Page 185

# Unintended Combos
# Odd Word Out 14

bad
sizes
on
rice

Answer on Page 186

# Unintended Combos
# Odd Word Out 15

drab
dean
owed
ride

Answer on Page 187

# Unintended Combos
# Odd Word Out 16

get
orb
tar
poles

Answer on Page 188

# Unintended Combos
# Odd Word Out 17

ants
see
ram
buck

Answer on Page 189

# Unintended Combos
## Odd Word Out 18

raw
lap
not
don

At least one of these words is backwards. At least one is not.

Answer on Page 190

# Cut-ins

Each puzzle in this chapter starts out as a familiar compound word or two-word phrase. Your challenge is to insert a word in-between its parts thereby creating two new compound words or two-word phrases.

For example, given the word

coffeecake

inserting the word *cup* produces

coffee cup cake

with the new combinations *coffee cup* and *cupcake.*

Mmm, for some reason I feel like taking a break and having a snack. You can take one too if you like.

# Cut-in 1

voice box
(4)

Answer on Page 191

# Cut-in 2

hat stand
(4)

Answer on Page 192

# Cut-in 3

overflow
(4)

Answer on Page 193

# Cut-in 4

airway
(5)

Answer on Page 194

# Cut-in 5

push-up
(3)

Answer on Page 195

# Cut-in 6

black box
(3)

Answer on Page 196

# Cut-in 7

lap dog
(3)

Answer on Page 197

# Cut-in 8

cross out
(3)

Answer on Page 198

# Cut-in 9

masterwork
(5)

Answer on Page 199

# Cut-in 10

double time
(8)

Answer on Page 200

# Cut-in 11

backhand
(3)

Answer on Page 201

# Cut-in 12

firearm
(4)

Answer on Page 202

# Cut-in 13

brain drain
(5)

Answer on Page 203

# Cut-in 14

horseback
(4)

Answer on Page 204

# Cut-in 15

food chain
(6)

Answer on Page 205

# Cut-in 16

bedroom
(4)

Answer on Page 206

# Cut-in 17

hole card
(5)

Answer on Page 207

# Cut-in 18

kitchen sink
(7)

Answer on Page 208

# Word Chain Loops

A word chain loop is a word chain that has no beginning or end; it forms a continuous circle. Start at any word and it will link to the words on each side, being the beginning of one compound word, two-word phrase or unintended combo and the end of another.

But to make the puzzles a bit more challenging, a synonym or antonym with the same number of letters is substituted for one of the actual words. I hope you're OK with this.

For example, replace one of these words with an antonym and make a 4-element chain loop:

exit
on
out
time

*Exit* is an antonym of *come*. The completed chain loop is

come-on
outcome        on time
time-out

Ready? Let's get loopy.

# Chain Loop 1

cold
out
hold
war

Answer on Page 209

# Chain Loop 2

cast
hand
bad
out

Answer on Page 210

# Chain Loop 3

front
rank
up
break

Answer on Page 211

# Chain Loop 4

out
set
spin
up

Answer on Page 212

# Chain Loop 5

end
off
up
zone

Answer on Page 213

# Chain Loop 6

base
boot
power
camp

Answer on Page 214

# Bonus Puzzles

Here are a few puzzles that didn't quite fit into the preceding chapters. I promise you'll get extra credit for each one that you solve.

Please note that any unintended combos in this chapter may have more than two component words. But every component word will have at least one letter—I promise.

# Bonus 1

Think of a word chain loop that consists of a fruit, a rift and an aide.

Answer on Page 215

# Bonus 2

What feature do these words and phrases have in common? Can you think of additional examples?

cake pan
lookout
outlay
racehorse

Answer on Page 216

# Bonus 3

What derogatory slang term for a wife also names two varieties of an atmospheric phenomenon?

Answer on Page 217

# Bonus 4

The list below has both genuine definitions and wacky definitions of five unintended combos. Match up the pairs of definitions and supply the unintended combos.

For example, *momentarily* and *cheese pest* define the unintended combo *briefly* (brie+fly).

display and flaunt
foot
garment edge
husk container
mild interjection
reflection
relate
skinny ruler
sprite painting
traditional story

Answer on Page 218

# Bonus 5

Assemble as many common 6-letter words as you can by using these 2-letter words like building blocks. Use each as many times as you want. My answer has four 6-letter words.

at
do
in
ma
or
to

Answer on Page 219

# Bonus 6

I hope this puzzle will not be an uphill struggle. You are given three words. Think of a compound word or two-word phrase that starts with the first given word. The second part of this word/phrase must have an opposite. Use that opposite as the first part of another compound word or two-word phrase. This, then, becomes the next step up the hill. Follow this procedure a total of (n) times to reach the third given word at the tippy top. Incorporate the second given word somewhere in-between.

For example, given *good, off, fat* (4), here is the resulting slope:

| | | | | |
|---|---|---|---|---|
| | | | low | fat |
| | | on | high | |
| | day | off | | |
| good | night | | | |

Now, scale the heights with *imminent, pitch, year* (4).

Answer on Page 220

# Bonus 7

This puzzle is like Bonus 6 but much, much easier because you'll be going downhill instead of uphill.

Think of a compound word or two-word phrase that starts with the first given word. Use the opposite of its second part as the first part of another compound word or two-word phrase. This becomes the next step down the hill. Follow this procedure a total of (n) times to reach the third given word at the bottom. Incorporate the second given word somewhere in-between.

For example, given *good, off, fat* (4), here is the resulting slope:

| | | | | |
|---|---|---|---|---|
| good | night | | | |
| | day | off | | |
| | | on | high | |
| | | | low | fat |

Stroll on down with *white, back, end* (4).

Answer on Page 221

# Bonus 8

Combine pairs of these eight synonyms/definitions to make four unintended combos. For example, you can merge *long story* with *incorporated municipality* to make *sagacity* (saga+city).

apt
commercial
deception
gentle tap
push out
relative
unrefined rock
wild disorder

Answer on Page 222

# Bonus 9

Insert a different capital city in the middle of each pair below then split the city at some point and use its parts to make new words. For example, inserting *London* between *gal* and *key* results in *gallon* and *donkey*.

| | |
|---|---|
| plum | early |
| jets | date |
| zig | ate |

Answer on Page 223

# Bonus 10

As in Bonus 9, insert a capital city in the middle of each pair of words, split the city at some point and use its parts to make new words. For example, and stop me if you've heard this one before, inserting *London* between *gal* and *key* gives you *gallon* and *donkey*.

Unlike Bonus 9, you'll have to discover the pairs yourself.

gray
let
par
place
plate
sure

Answer on Page 224

## Bonus 11

Pair up these six words such that when you supply the missing middle words you create three different 2-element word chains.

For example, given *card* and *lamp*, you can supply *post* to create this short chain: *lamppost postcard*.

trade
time
delivery
guard
powder
pipe

Answer on Page 225

# Bonus 12

Use all but two of these small words as building blocks to answer the three questions below. Each answer consists of at least two unintended combos.

| | | | | |
|---|---|---|---|---|
| am | an | be | ends | |
| king | ma | me | pa | pal |
| per | pin | sis | the | to |

1. What is a good source of folate, magnesium and phosphorous?

2. What sometimes happens after committing a wrong?

3. What is an important student document?

Answer on Page 226

# Bonus 13

Assemble as many 9-letter words as you can using these 3-letter words as building blocks. Use each as many times as you want. My answer has four 9-letter words.

son
age
ant
ate
med
con
for
per

Answer on Page 227

# Bonus 14

Your goal here is to connect three compound words (or two-word phrases) into a single chain. Change a single letter of one's second part to make the first part of the next one in the chain.

For example, by changing *chuck* to *check* you link *woodchuck* to *checkmate* and by changing *mate* to *make* you then link *checkmate* to *make-believe.*

woodchuck   checkmate   make-believe

Use only three of these hints/definitions to create the chain.

brittle cookie
faithful's conflict
spot for rendezvous
ring location

Answer on Page 228

# Bonus 15

This puzzle is similar to Bonus 14 except that you'll be connecting three unintended combos instead of ordinary compound words. Change one letter of a combo's last component to make the first component of the next combo in the chain.

For example, by changing *era* to *err* you link *camera* to *errand* and by changing *and* to *end* you then link *errand* to *endowed.*

camera errand endowed

Use only three of these synonyms/definitions to create the chain.

depict again
grounds
spoiled
tracts

Answer on Page 229

# About the Author

Mark Van Horne is a vibrant, discerning and erudite man who is not afraid to use his powers of exaggeration when writing about himself. His love of word puzzles began in his adolescence. A relentless reader of almost anything other than his textbooks, he eventually realized that language is simply chock-a-block with peculiar combinations, multiple meanings, weird spellings and lots of other neat stuff.

Nowadays, much to his surprise, Mark has a job. He lives in Honolulu with his wife and high-speed Internet service.

# Hints

# Fill-in 1 Hint

summer treat

Page 12

# Fill-in 2 Hint

spa scene

Page 13

# Fill-in 3 Hint

give little weight to

Page 14

# Fill-in 4 Hint

digs for plants

Page 15

# Fill-in 5 Hint

spirit costume

Page 16

# Fill-in 6 Hint

produce spot

Page 17

# Fill-in 7 Hint

Congratulations, you have found the hidden puzzle! Make a very short phrase of unintended combos from these words:

at
con
disco
firm
ion
very

# Answers

# Make a Chain 1 Answer

otherwise wisecrack crackpot potpie

Page 2

# Make a Chain 2 Answer

Page 3

soda pop popcorn corn silk silkworm

# Make a Chain 3 Answer

Page 4

brown sugar sugar cube cube root root cellar

# Make a Chain 4 Answer

salt mine mine field field hand handball

Page 5

# Make a Chain 5 Answer

anyone one-way wayside side road

Page 6

# Make a Chain 6 Answer

Page 7

oh so so there therefor forbear

# Make a Chain 7 Answer

cutback backup up-front front runner

lie low lowdown downright right angle

Page 8

# Make a Chain 8 Answer

stopover overturn turnover overeat

Page 9

# Make a Chain 9 Answer

underhand handhold holdover over par

Page 10

# Fill-in 1 Answer

ice cream

dry ice   ice cold   cold cream   creampuff

Page 12

# Fill-in 2 Answer

hot spring

red-hot hotbed bedspring spring break

Page 13

# Fill-in 3 Answer

downplay

touchdown down under underplay playmate

Page 14

# Fill-in 4 Answer

greenhouse

wintergreen green tea teahouse housebroken

Page 15

# Fill-in 5 Answer

bedsheet

flowerbed bedspread spreadsheet sheet music

Page 16

# Fill-in 6 Answer

farm stand

fish farm farmhand handstand stand pat

Page 17

# Fill-in 7 Answer

bucktooth

sawbuck buckeye eyetooth toothpaste

Page 18

# Fill-in 8 Answer

laptop

overlap lap desk desktop top hat

Page 19

# Fill-in 9 Answer

card game

face card cardboard board game game point

Page 20

# Fill-in 10 Answer

Page 21

midnight sun sunspot spotlight lightweight

sunlight

# Fill-in 11 Answer

open bar

wide-open   open space   space bar   barcode

Page 22

# Fill-in 12 Answer

kick off

sidekick kickstand standoff offshoot

Page 23

# Unintended Combo
# Fill-in 1 Answer

funding dingbat bathe heart

Page 27

# Unintended Combo
# Fill-in 2 Answer

Page 28

seethe theme meant anthem

# Unintended Combo
## Fill-in 3 Answer

Page 29

rampant panther herbed bedevil

# Unintended Combo
# Fill-in 4 Answer

carrot rotten tenor orate

Page 30

# Unintended Combo
## Fill-in 5 Answer

capstan tandoors doorstops topsoil

Page 31

# Unintended Combo
# Fill-in 6 Answer

dodo dome meme merely

Page 32

# Odd Word Out 1 Answer

out: north
companion: watch

watchdog
stopwatch
watchtower

Page 34

# Odd Word Out 2 Answer

out: pipe
companion: cell

fuel cell
cellblock
stem cell

Page 35

# Odd Word Out 3 Answer

My intended answer is

out: milk
companion: tool

toolbar
toolbox
power tool

An alternate answer is

out: box
companion: man

barman
milkman
manpower

Page 36

# Odd Word Out 4 Answer

out: park
companion: base

baseball
database
baseline

Page 37

# Odd Word Out 5 Answer

out: catch
companion: slide

landslide
mudslide
slideshow

Page 38

# Odd Word Out 6 Answer

out: barrel
companion: search

search engine
search party
strip-search

Page 39

# Odd Word Out 7 Answer

out: muscle

companion: broken

broken-down
heartbroken
housebroken

Page 40

# Odd Word Out 8 Answer

out: time
companion: bird

birdbath
birdbrain
jailbird

Page 41

# Odd Word Out 9 Answer

out: cow

companion: hat

hard-hat
straw hat
hat trick

Page 42

# Odd Word Out 10 Answer

out: stone
companion: paper

flypaper
sandpaper
paperweight

Page 43

# Odd Word Out 11 Answer

out: key
companion: rib

rib eye
prime rib
sparerib

Page 44

# Odd Word Out 12 Answer

out: ranch
companion: fever

hay fever
fever pitch
yellow fever

Page 45

# Odd Word Out 13 Answer

out: party
companion: model

model home
fashion model
working model

Page 46

# Odd Word Out 14 Answer

out: wick
companion: ball

mothball
ball gown
fireball

Page 47

# Odd Word Out 15 Answer

out: magic
companion: horse

quarter horse
horseback
horse sense

Page 48

# Odd Word Out 16 Answer

out: test
companion: land

mainland
crash-land
landlady

Page 49

# Odd Word Out 17 Answer

out: yard
companion: mail

chain mail
fan mail
mail-order

Page 50

# Odd Word Out 18 Answer

out: shark
companion: track

track meet
soundtrack
off-track

Page 51

# Unintended Combo
# Odd Word Out 1 Answer

out: has
companion: try

pantry
tapestry
trysting

Page 54

# Unintended Combo Odd Word Out 2 Answer

out: or
companion: on

lesson
onus
soon

Page 55

# Unintended Combo
# Odd Word Out 3 Answer

out: fit

companion: ear

earnest
earthen
endear

Page 56

# Unintended Combo
# Odd Word Out 4 Answer

out: set
companion: gas

bodegas
gasping
togas

Page 57

# Unintended Combo
# Odd Word Out 5 Answer

out: he
companion: go

gosling
mango
tango

Page 58

# Unintended Combo
# Odd Word Out 6 Answer

out: tin
companion: ice

cornice
justice
office

Page 59

# Unintended Combo
# Odd Word Out 7 Answer

out: post
companion: bled

humbled
stubbled
warbled

Page 60

# Unintended Combo
# Odd Word Out 8 Answer

out: cat
companion: row

furrow
rowdies
sparrow

Page 61

# Unintended Combo
# Odd Word Out 9 Answer

out: ton
companion: men

menace
menswear
mentally

Page 62

# Unintended Combo
# Odd Word Out 10 Answer

out: dam
companion: old

mistold
outsold
threshold

Page 63

# Unintended Combo
# Odd Word Out 11 Answer

out: sins
companion: rein

reinforce
reinvest
therein

Page 64

# Unintended Combo
# Odd Word Out 12 Answer

out: amen
companion: rest

rearrest
restitch
sincerest

Page 65

# Unintended Combo
# Odd Word Out 13 Answer

out: let
companion: imp

impact
impeach
improve

Page 66

# Unintended Combo
# Odd Word Out 14 Answer

out: bad
companion: cap

capon
caprice
capsizes

Page 67

# Unintended Combo
# Odd Word Out 15 Answer

out: dean
companion: best

bestowed
bestride
drabbest

Page 68

# Unintended Combo
# Odd Word Out 16 Answer

out: orb
companion: tar

polestar
target
tartar

Page 69

# Unintended Combo
# Odd Word Out 17 Answer

out: buck
companion: page

pageants
rampage
seepage

Page 70

# Unintended Combo
# Odd Word Out 18 Answer

out: raw
companion: ate

donate
notate
palate

Page 71

# Cut-in 1 Answer

voice mail    mailbox

Page 74

# Cut-in 2 Answer

hatband    bandstand

Page 75

# Cut-in 3 Answer

overwork workflow

Page 76

# Cut-in 4 Answer

airspeed speedway

Page 77

# Cut-in 5 Answer

pushpin pinup

Page 78

# Cut-in 6 Answer

black ice icebox

Page 79

# Cut-in 7 Answer

laptop    top dog

Page 80

# Cut-in 8 Answer

crossbow    bow out

Page 81

# Cut-in 9 Answer

masterpiece piecework

Page 82

# Cut-in 10 Answer

double standard    standard time

Page 83

# Cut-in 11 Answer

back off offhand

Page 84

# Cut-in 12 Answer

fireside sidearm

Page 85

# Cut-in 13 Answe

Page 86

brainstorm storm drain

# Cut-in 14 Answer

horseplay    playback

Page 87

# Cut-in 15 Answer

food supply    supply chain

Page 88

# Cut-in 16 Answer

bed rest restroom

Page 89

# Cut-in 17 Answer

hole punch    punch card

Page 90

# Cut-in 18 Answer

kitchen counter     countersink

# Chain Loop 1 Answer

hold ... lock

lockout

warlock out cold

cold war

Page 94

# Chain Loop 2 Answer

bad ... off

offhand

castoff handout

outcast

Page 95

# Chain Loop 3 Answer

rank ... line

line break

front line breakup

up-front

Page 96

# Chain Loop 4 Answer

spin ... turn

turnout

upturn outset

setup

Page 97

# Chain Loop 5 Answer

zone ... ward

ward off

upward offend

end up

Page 98

# Chain Loop 6 Answer

boot ... fire

firepower

campfire    power base

base camp

Page 99

# Bonus 1 Answer

banana

second split

Page 102

# Bonus 2 Answer

New words and phrases are made when these are read „backwards:"

| | |
|---|---|
| cake pan | pancake |
| look out | outlook |
| outlay | layout |
| racehorse | horse race |

Page 103

# Bonus 3 Answer

Ball and chain. (lightning)

Page 104

# Bonus 4 Answer

Page 105

display and flaunt & husk container = brandish
traditional story & foot = legend
mild interjection & garment edge = ahem
reflection & skinny ruler = thinking
relate & sprite painting = impart

# Bonus 5 Answer

domain
indoor
orator
tomato

Page 106

# Bonus 6 Answer

light year
pitch dark
safety catch
imminent danger

Page 107

# Bonus 7 Answer

white hot
cold front
back down
up end

Page 108

# Bonus 8 Answer

commercial + unrefined rock = adore
deception + apt = confit
gentle tap + wild disorder = patriot
push out + relative = pumpkin

Page 109

# Bonus 9 Answer

plumber Berlin linearly
jetsam Amman mandate
zigzag Zagreb rebate

Page 110

# Bonus 10 Answer

parka Kabul bullet
placebos Boston tonsure
plateau Austin stingray

Page 111

# Bonus 11 Answer

With my apologies...

| | | |
|---|---|---|
| trade | mark | time |
| delivery | van | guard |
| powder | horn | pipe |

Page 112

# Bonus 12 Answer

1. pinto bean
2. making amends
3. thesis paper

# Bonus 13 Answer

consonant
perforate
performed
personage

Page 114

# Bonus 14 Answer

holy war
ear lobe
love nest

Page 115

# Bonus 15 Answer

redraw red raw
rationale rat ion ale
areas are as

Page 116

Printed in the USA
CPSIA information can be obtained
at www.ICGtesting.com
LVHW011740021223
765401LV00004B/275

9 780971 422131